Ivy Global

MW00620910

SSAT & ISEE

VOCABULARY 2, EDITION 2.0

MADE WITH CARE

NEW YORK

This publication was written and edited by the team at Ivy Global.

Editors: Sacha Azor and Natalia Irizarry-Cole

Producers: Lloyd Min and Junho Suh

Contributors: Alexandra Candib, Lei Huang, Amelia McLeod, Yolanda Song, and Adam Wolsky

About Ivy Global

Ivy Global is a pioneering education company that produces high-quality educational material.

E-mail: publishing@ivyglobal.com
Website: http://www.ivyglobal.com

Introduction

Welcome, students and parents! This pocketbook is intended to help students prepare for the level of vocabulary encountered on the SSAT & ISEE. For students applying to many top private and independent schools in North America, these exams are a crucial and sometimes daunting step in the admissions process. By helping you master these core vocabulary words, Ivy Global will help you build your confidence and maximize your score on these important exams.

Comprehensive Prep

We know that no two students are exactly alike—each student brings unique personal strengths to his or her test preparation. For this reason, we've tailored our preparation materials to help students with a specific subject area or goal. Ivy Global also offers full sets of SSAT and ISEE books to help students develop the best strategies for each section of these exams:

- *SSAT English, SSAT Math, SSAT Practice*
- *ISEE English, ISEE Math, ISEE Practice*

This book is the second in a set of three vocabulary pocketbooks for the SSAT and ISEE that include a total of 365 words for every-day learning:

- *Vocabulary 1* (Essential) – Words 1-125
- *Vocabulary 2* (Extended) – Words 126-250
- *Vocabulary 3* (Advanced) – Words 251-365

Ivy Global's products are available for purchase at ivyglobal.com/products or amazon.com.

How to Use This Book

This book is a study aid; it isn't a complete dictionary. The words here are selected because they are likely to be useful when studying for the SSAT and ISEE, and we've given brief definitions to help you quickly learn the most common meaning of each word. There is more information available about each word, including information about less common definitions and the history and etymology of each word.

- When you learn a word, pay attention to its part of speech (is it a noun, verb, adjective, or adverb?) and look for other possible definitions of the word.
- Be sure to write your own personal sentence for each word to help you remember it.
- When you're writing your sentence, if you don't totally understand the meaning of a word you should try to search for other sentences containing the word.
- Use a pencil, and have a trusted reader check your sentences.
- Correct your sentences if you don't quite capture the meanings of the words on your first try.
- In order to master as many words as possible before your exam, create a daily schedule and make sure to review old words while you are learning new ones.

Sample Study Schedule

To begin, try using this sample study plan as a model for your own personalized study schedule.

Sample Study Schedule		
Week	Words this Week	Goal Reached?
1	1 - 25	☐
2	26 - 50	☐
3	51 - 75	☐
4	76 - 100	☐
5	101 – 125	☐
6	Final Review	☐

We recommend focusing on 10-40 words each week. The table above is for a schedule of learning 25 words per week.

Learning New Words

As you work through these vocabulary words, make sure that you're using the most effective strategies.

Use mnemonics: Mnemonics are devices to help improve your memory and can be used to help you remember difficult words. They can use combinations of words, images, patterns of letters or a myriad of other things. Mnemonic devices should only be used with words that are complex—short, easy to remember words can actually become more complicated with the use of a mnemonic device. Mnemonics help you convert abstract information into a mix of what you already know.

You can use similar sounding words to remember a new one:

- There are no sirens in this serene neighborhood.

Siren is something that is loud and annoying, but serene means "calm and clear." A lack of sirens will make for a serene environment.

- The wrecking ball was raised to raze the building.

Raze means "destroy," and a wrecking ball would probably get the job done.

You can also use something more visual:

- Novel tea would be a novelty. Usually tea is made from plants, not books!

Expand your classroom: Don't think of learning vocabulary as something you need to do just for the SSAT or ISEE. Instead, try to make these words a part of your everyday life. There are lots of creative ways you can use your new vocabulary words:

- Start using the words you learn in essays and homework assignments.
- Try making a tricky word your theme for an art project.
- Use new words in conversations with friends and family.
- Tape flash cards or put sticky notes with the words you're learning around your house and recite the definition of a word each time you see it.
- Compete with your friends to see who can master the most words.
- Draw a picture that captures the meaning of a word.

Know Connotations: A word's connotation is its secondary meaning, or the feeling we get from the word. A word can have a positive (+) connotation if it means something good, a negative (-) connotation if it means something bad, or a neutral connotation if it is neither good nor bad.

For example, the word "horrible" has a negative connotation, whereas "joyous" has a positive connotation. If you can remember that a word means something positive or negative, you may be able to eliminate answer choices with the opposite connotation if you encounter them on your exam.

Come up with contexts: If you want to remember multiple definitions of a word, one useful strategy is to come up with many contexts—phrases where you might have heard the word before. A word's context is everything in a phrase or sentence that might influence the word's meaning. The word "charge," for example can have many different meanings, depending on its context. It might be helpful to make yourself a bubble chart and think of as many phrases as you can:

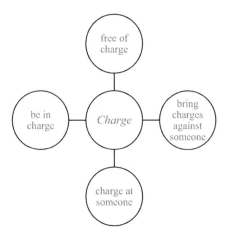

What does "charge" mean in each of these contexts? "Free of charge" means that you don't have to pay for something; to "be in charge" means to have power or be in control; to "charge at someone" means to attack suddenly or assault; and to "bring charges against someone" means to accuse or blame.

Let's begin!

accommodate

fulfill the needs
or wishes of (v)

Our kitchen staff will be happy to accommodate any dietary restrictions you may have.

Your sentence:

_____

_____

_____

_____

_____

_____

acknowledge

recognize or admit as true (v)

He acknowledged that he had not treated his friends very well.

Your sentence:

_____

_____

_____

_____

_____

_____

affliction

something which causes pain or misery (n)

Asthma can be a serious affliction, especially in areas with a lot of air pollution.

Your sentence:

_____

_____

_____

_____

_____

_____

agile

quick and easy in movement or thought (adj)

Football players sometimes take ballet classes to help them become agile as well as strong.

Your sentence:

_____

_____

_____

_____

_____

_____

amiable

friendly; sociable; good-natured (adj)

I was nervous about my new job, but my amiable supervisor put me at ease right away.

Your sentence:

_____

_____

_____

_____

_____

_____

amnesty

full forgiveness or pardon for offenses (n)

Although he had been found guilty of serious crimes, he was granted amnesty by the president.

Your sentence:

_____

_____

_____

_____

_____

_____

appease

achieve a sense of peace by giving into someone's desires (v)

I don't like taking out my nose ring, but I do it to appease my father.

Your sentence:

_____

_____

_____

_____

_____

_____

astute

perceptive; sharp
in thought (adj)

The general's astute analysis of the opposing
army's weaknesses led his country to victory.

Your sentence:

_____

_____

_____

_____

_____

_____

autonomous

able to act independently (adj)

While Puerto Rico is not a state, it is also not an autonomous nation, as the United States makes decisions concerning its finances.

Your sentence:

_____

_____

_____

_____

_____

_____

baffling

very confusing (adj)

She was generally very polite, so her rudeness at dinner was baffling to her parents.

Your sentence:

_____

_____

_____

_____

_____

_____

beneficial

helpful; useful (adj)

If you're aiming for high grades, a good night's sleep can be more beneficial than staying up late cramming.

Your sentence:

_____

_____

_____

_____

_____

_____

beseech

ask urgently (v)

I beseech you: turn that terrible music down!

Your sentence:

_____

_____

_____

_____

_____

_____

blatant

obvious (adj)

I couldn't believe he was trying to fool me with such a blatant lie.

Your sentence:

_____

_____

_____

_____

_____

_____

blemish

an imperfection (n); ruin the appearance of something (v)

Her occasional tardiness was the only blemish on her otherwise stellar work performance.

Your sentence:

_____

_____

_____

_____

_____

_____

boon

something helpful (n)

The charitable donations we receive are a major boon to our program.

Your sentence:

_____

_____

_____

_____

_____

_____

brink

the edge of something steep; the point before something bad happens (n)

He was on the brink of losing his temper, but he managed to stay calm.

Your sentence:

_____

_____

_____

_____

_____

_____

calamity

disaster (n)

Scientists think the calamity that caused the dinosaurs to become extinct was related to a meteor that hit the earth.

Your sentence:

_____

_____

_____

_____

_____

_____

candid

honest;
straightforward (adj)

Voters were drawn to her because she seemed unusually candid for a politician.

Your sentence:

_____

_____

_____

_____

_____

_____

charismatic

having a compelling presence (adj)

He was famous for being a charismatic speaker who could attract crowds as large as five thousand people.

Your sentence:

_____

_____

_____

_____

_____

_____

cleave

split or sever (v)

After practicing karate for many years, he was finally able to cleave a wooden board with the stroke of his hand.

Your sentence:

_____

_____

_____

_____

_____

_____

coalesce

come together (v)

She had several good ideas for her essay, but she was struggling to make them coalesce into a unified whole.

Your sentence:

_____

_____

_____

_____

_____

_____

coerce

use force or threats to make someone do something (v)

The judge ruled that the defendant had been coerced into allowing the robbers into the bank and therefore was innocent.

Your sentence:

_____

_____

_____

_____

_____

_____

colossal

huge (adj)

His colossal error cost the company several million dollars.

Your sentence:

_____

_____

_____

_____

_____

_____

condemn

disapprove of (v)

Marco condemned his school's practice of throwing out, rather than donating or recycling, extra school supplies.

Your sentence:

_____

_____

_____

_____

_____

_____

contradict

say the opposite of something (v)

Although he had promised to create new jobs, the CEO contradicted his previous statements by letting 5,000 people go.

Your sentence:

_____

_____

_____

_____

_____

_____

contrite

showing remorse (adj)

After the family discovered that Fido ate the food off the table, their anger quickly subsided as they noticed the contrite look on Fido's face.

Your sentence:

_____

_____

_____

_____

_____

_____

convoluted

unnecessarily complicated (adj)

The teacher was forced to take points off of Georgia's exam because her convoluted answers were difficult to understand.

Your sentence:

_____

_____

_____

_____

_____

_____

corrupt

dishonest, tainted (adj)

The corrupt police officer accepted the criminal's bribe.

Your sentence:

_____

_____

_____

_____

_____

_____

crusade

campaign to defend an idea or cause (n); lead or take part in such a campaign (v)

The environmentalists went on a crusade against plastic bags.

Your sentence:

_____

_____

_____

_____

_____

_____

debate

argument (n)

The teachers held a debate about the effectiveness of using computers in their classrooms.

Your sentence:

_____

_____

_____

_____

_____

_____

debilitate

weaken (v)

The basketball team was debilitated by the absence of their star guard.

Your sentence:

_____

_____

_____

_____

_____

_____

debunk

show something is false (v)

Copernicus and Galileo debunked the myth that the sun revolved around the Earth.

Your sentence:

_____

_____

_____

_____

_____

_____

delineate

describe precisely (v)

Thomas made sure to carefully delineate the boundaries of his property after his neighbor's dog entered his yard several times.

Your sentence:

_____

_____

_____

_____

_____

_____

delude

trick, deceive (v)

The savvy car salesmen was able to delude
Patrick into buying a used car for nearly twice
what it was worth.

Your sentence:

_____

_____

_____

_____

_____

_____

devious

underhanded; skillfully dishonest; crooked (adj)

The devious politician was elected based on promises he never intended to keep.

Your sentence:

_____

_____

_____

_____

_____

_____

doubt

be uncertain about (v);
uncertainty (n)

Jonathan doubted his daughter's story, which was full of inconsistencies.

Your sentence:

_____

_____

_____

_____

_____

_____

eccentric

odd; strange (adj)

Her neighbors thought Tamara was eccentric; she rarely left her house and had at least 15 cats living with her.

Your sentence:

_____

_____

_____

_____

_____

_____

elite

exclusive (adj)

The Ivy League universities are considered among the most elite universities in the United States.

Your sentence:

_____

_____

_____

_____

_____

_____

empathy

the ability to share someone's emotions (n)

When David lost his job, his wife Pilar felt empathy for him, having gone through that experience just a year before.

Your sentence:

_____

_____

_____

_____

_____

_____

encumber

cause problems; burden (v)

The suitcase encumbered the man as he tried to fit into the very full subway car.

Your sentence:

_____

_____

_____

_____

_____

_____

erode

disintegrate (v)

Years of harsh winds from tropical storms and hurricanes have eroded the Louisiana coast.

Your sentence:

_____

_____

_____

_____

_____

_____

eschew

avoid, shun (v)

Marianne eschewed going out on weekends in favor of getting sleep.

Your sentence:

_____

_____

_____

_____

_____

_____

exhilarate

excite (v)

The visit to the candy shop exhilarated the children.

Your sentence:

_____

_____

_____

_____

_____

_____

exile

Ivy Global

banish (v)

The spies were exiled from the country when the authorities found out what they were doing.

Your sentence:

_____

_____

_____

_____

_____

_____

exploit

take advantage of (v)

The Spanish exploited the natural resources of Mexico, using slaves and indigenous workers to mine silver while keeping the profits for the crown of Spain.

Your sentence:

_____

_____

_____

_____

_____

_____

extol

praise highly (v)

Gandhi has long been extolled for his non-violent protest against British colonial rule in India.

Your sentence:

_____

_____

_____

_____

_____

_____

extract

remove (v)

The dentist extracted the patient's wisdom teeth in order to prevent future tooth decay.

Your sentence:

_____

_____

_____

_____

_____

_____

fallacy

a false idea or belief (n)

Opponents to feminism have always supported their arguments with a number of commonly accepted fallacies.

Your sentence:

_____

_____

_____

_____

_____

_____

falter

stumble, hesitate (v)

His voice often faltered when he spoke in front of large groups of people.

Your sentence:

_____

_____

_____

_____

_____

_____

fatigue

weariness, exhaustion (n)

I was overcome with fatigue after the 22-hour flight to Australia.

Your sentence:

_____

_____

_____

_____

_____

_____

fickle

inconstant, unreliable, frequently changing (adj)

He was a fickle boy whose taste in toys was frequently changing.

Your sentence:

_____

_____

_____

_____

_____

_____

fissure

narrow opening or crack; division (n)

Her phone survived the fall, but the screen was left with several long fissures.

Your sentence:

_____

_____

_____

_____

_____

_____

fluctuate

increase and decrease in amount (v)

In October the temperature fluctuates so much that it's hard to dress appropriately for the weather.

Your sentence:

_____

_____

_____

_____

_____

_____

fortify

strengthen (v)

During the flu season, I fortify my body with vitamins, plenty of sleep, and warm clothing.

Your sentence:

_____

_____

_____

_____

_____

_____

gimmick

a publicity trick (n)

The contest was nothing but a gimmick to increase sales.

Your sentence:

_____

_____

_____

_____

_____

_____

havoc

destruction, devastation; chaos (n)

The hurricane wreaked havoc over my hometown.

Your sentence:

_____

_____

_____

_____

_____

_____

hubris

Ivy Global

excessive pride or self-confidence (n)

The general's hubris made him underestimate the strength of his opponents, which led to his downfall.

Your sentence:

_____

_____

_____

_____

_____

_____

illuminate

cast light on; clarify (v)

During the holiday season, the street was illuminated by strings of lights.

Your sentence:

_____

_____

_____

_____

_____

_____

incentive

motive, inducement (n)

His parents offered to make his favorite meal as an incentive for doing his share of chores.

Your sentence:

_____

_____

_____

_____

_____

_____

indifferent

uninterested,
apathetic (adj)

She was required to take an advanced science class, but was indifferent as to which one.

Your sentence:

_____

_____

_____

_____

_____

_____

inhabit

live in, occupy (v)

Badgers inhabited the forest behind his house.

Your sentence:

_____

_____

_____

_____

_____

_____

intervene

come between,
become involved (v)

When the students appeared to be on the verge of a fight, the teacher intervened.

Your sentence:

_____

_____

_____

_____

_____

_____

intrinsic

inherent, inborn, essential (adj)

Critics of affirmative action often fail to see the intrinsic value of a diverse classroom or workplace.

Your sentence:

_____

_____

_____

_____

_____

_____

irate

very angry (adj)

The chef felt his cooking had been unfairly criticized in the restaurant review, so he left the reviewer a number of irate messages.

Your sentence:

_____

_____

_____

_____

_____

_____

jeopardize

endanger (v)

Drunk drivers jeopardize the safety of everyone on the road.

Your sentence:

_____

_____

_____

_____

_____

_____

keen

enthusiastic; highly developed (adj)

Dogs tend to be good hunters because of their keen sense of smell.

Your sentence:

_____

_____

_____

_____

_____

_____

lethal

fatal, deadly, murderous (adj)

The venom of the black widow spider can be lethal if a bite is left untreated.

Your sentence:

_____

_____

_____

_____

_____

_____

lush

luxuriant, abundant, rich (adj)

The lush forest was home to a wide diversity of species.

Your sentence:

_____

_____

_____

_____

_____

_____

magnanimous

generous (adj)

She was magnanimous in forgiving the petty remarks her friend had made when he was envious of the attention she received.

Your sentence:

_____

_____

_____

_____

_____

_____

mandate

official order (n)

The governor's mandate to build more schools was well-received by her constituents.

Your sentence:

_____

_____

_____

_____

_____

_____

meager

scant, inadequate (adj)

Those meager portions of food will barely keep us from starving!

Your sentence:

_____

_____

_____

_____

_____

_____

meek

submissive, timid (adj)

Although she seemed meek at first, I soon found that she was quite vocal about her opinions.

Your sentence:

_____

_____

_____

_____

_____

_____

memento

an object kept
as a reminder (n)

He was a sentimental person who liked to keep
mementos from all his past relationships.

Your sentence:

_____

_____

_____

_____

_____

_____

metaphor

comparative figure of speech, analogy (n)

Her use of imaginative metaphors rendered her writing both informative and interesting.

Your sentence:

_____

_____

_____

_____

_____

_____

meticulous

thorough, conscientious (adj)

She performed excellently on exams because she took meticulous notes in class.

Your sentence:

_____

_____

_____

_____

_____

_____

mute

unable or unwilling
to speak; silent (adj)

The mute woman had to testify in court by
writing down her answers.

Your sentence:

_____

_____

_____

_____

_____

_____

nascent

new; beginning
to develop (adj)

The nascent company at first had difficulties marketing their product, but eventually they found success.

Your sentence:

_____

_____

_____

_____

_____

_____

novelty

something new
and unusual (n)

The iPhone was a novelty when it first came out,
but smart phones have now become the norm.

Your sentence:

_____

_____

_____

_____

_____

_____

orate

speak pretentiously (v)

The candidate's tendency to orate turned off voters, ultimately costing him the election.

Your sentence:

_____

_____

_____

_____

_____

_____

orderly

organized (adj)

Jonathan's room was surprisingly orderly for a teenager's bedroom, with only a bit of clutter on his desk.

Your sentence:

_____

_____

_____

_____

_____

_____

ornate

elaborate; showy (adj)

The Jeffersons' ornate Christmas decorations bothered their neighbors.

Your sentence:

_____

_____

_____

_____

_____

_____

pandemonium

chaos (n)

It was pandemonium in the town hall after the people found out that their representative had been using the taxpayers' money to fund lavish vacations.

Your sentence:

_____

_____

_____

_____

_____

_____

perplex

confuse (v)

The feeling of love perplexed the android, for it seemed illogical and irrational to its robotic programming.

Your sentence:

_____

_____

_____

_____

_____

_____

philanthropy

charity (n)

Bill Gates' philanthropy has provided millions of people access to anti-malaria pills.

Your sentence:

_____

_____

_____

_____

_____

_____

piety

devotion (n)

The widow's religious piety became more pronounced after her husband passed away.

Your sentence:

_____

_____

_____

_____

_____

_____

pilot

drive (v)

Despite his experience, the captain of the ship piloted the vessel into an iceberg.

Your sentence:

_____

_____

_____

_____

_____

_____

plead

beg (v)

Georgia pleaded with her teacher for a better grade, but her teacher refused to change it.

Your sentence:

_____

_____

_____

_____

_____

_____

plight

misfortune (n)

The family's plight began when they lost their home in a flood.

Your sentence:

_____

_____

_____

_____

_____

_____

prohibit

ban, outlaw (v)

The consumption and sale of alcohol was
prohibited in the United States during the 1920s.

Your sentence:

_____

_____

_____

_____

_____

_____

prudent

wise, careful (adj)

It is prudent to wear your seat belt when you are in a car in case you get into an accident.

Your sentence:

_____

_____

_____

_____

_____

_____

qualm

unease, uncertainty (n)

Sarah had qualms about going to university in Boston, having grown up in the hot desert of Arizona.

Your sentence:

_____

_____

_____

_____

_____

_____

quixotic

foolishly optimistic (adj)

The short man's dream of being a professional basketball player was a quixotic pursuit.

Your sentence:

_____

_____

_____

_____

_____

_____

rank

level in organization (n)

He went up in rank in the police force after his heroic save of Sergeant Franklin.

Your sentence:

_____

_____

_____

_____

_____

_____

recede

move back (v)

After the storm caused massive floods, the water began to recede when the rain stopped.

Your sentence:

_____

_____

_____

_____

_____

_____

remote

far-off, isolated (adj)

The village was in a remote part of the Yukon, only accessible by traveling on dirt roads.

Your sentence:

_____

_____

_____

_____

_____

_____

renovate

fix, restore (v)

The building was renovated after part of the roof collapsed.

Your sentence:

_____

_____

_____

_____

_____

_____

renown

fame, acclaim (n)

Her critically acclaimed novel brought her renown among fans of literature but not very much money.

Your sentence:

_____

_____

_____

_____

_____

_____

reproach

disapprove, blame (v)

Stacy reproached her son after she found him cheating on his homework.

Your sentence:

_____

_____

_____

_____

_____

_____

righteous

moral, virtuous (adj)

The righteous woman gave the homeless man
her bag of groceries.

Your sentence:

_____

_____

_____

_____

_____

_____

rigor

exactness or preciseness (n)

The scientist conducted his experiments with rigor, making sure to follow every step exactly.

Your sentence:

_____

_____

_____

_____

_____

_____

scarce

limited; hard to find (adj)

During World War II, some foods were scarce and required rationing.

Your sentence:

_____

_____

_____

_____

_____

_____

schism

division (n)

A schism developed between the two owners of the company because they had differences of opinion on the project.

Your sentence:

_____

_____

_____

_____

_____

_____

scrutiny

critical observation (n)

Jamie's teacher criticized almost every sentence of his essay, making him feel like he was under extreme scrutiny.

Your sentence:

_____

_____

_____

_____

_____

_____

sever

divide; end a relationship (v)

She wanted to sever all ties with her business partner because he was driving away potential clients.

Your sentence:

_____

_____

_____

_____

_____

_____

skirmish

a small fight (n)

Their skirmish probably would have become a full-blown brawl if a teacher hadn't interrupted them.

Your sentence:

_____

_____

_____

_____

_____

_____

somber

dark or dull (adj)

As Alex sat in the park, she noticed that the overcast winter sky was somber, almost lifeless.

Your sentence:

_____

_____

_____

_____

_____

_____

squander

waste something (v)

He decided to never squander the wealth his family had worked so hard to accumulate.

Your sentence:

_____

_____

_____

_____

_____

_____

stamina

endurance (n)

She had the stamina to work all night to meet the new deadline.

Your sentence:

_____

_____

_____

_____

_____

_____

stark

severe; harsh (adj)

The stark reality was that she would not have enough time for both gymnastics and orchestra.

Your sentence:

_____

_____

_____

_____

_____

_____

strenuous

requiring or displaying great effort (adj)

The doctor told him to avoid all strenuous movements until his back is fully healed.

Your sentence:

_____

_____

_____

_____

_____

_____

subdue

bring under control (v)

The police officer had to subdue the suspect by tackling and handcuffing him.

Your sentence:

_____

_____

_____

_____

_____

_____

surpass

outperform; beat (v)

The amount of money raised is anticipated to surpass last year's total.

Your sentence:

_____

_____

_____

_____

_____

_____

tangible

able to be felt (adj)

He didn't just want the plans for the new toy; he wanted something tangible that he could actually hold in his hands.

Your sentence:

_____

_____

_____

_____

_____

_____

thorough

complete (adj)

She was very thorough in checking that every strap was tightly fastened because the last time the family took a trip, the canoe fell off the top of the car.

Your sentence:

_____

_____

_____

_____

_____

_____

tranquil

free from
disturbance (adj)

The house felt tranquil after everyone left the party.

Your sentence:

_____

_____

_____

_____

_____

_____

truce

an agreement to stop fighting (n)

The two countries reached a truce to end the war.

Your sentence:

_____

_____

_____

_____

_____

_____

umbrage

offense, annoyance (n)

He took umbrage at the implication that he was unprepared for the rigors of scientific research.

Your sentence:

_____

_____

_____

_____

_____

_____

uproar

chaos; outcry (n)

There was uproar in the classroom when the teacher assigned extra homework.

Your sentence:

_____

_____

_____

_____

_____

_____

vigor

strength, energy, determination (n)

Aatiyah was voted team captain because of her great vigor and devotion.

Your sentence:

_____

_____

_____

_____

_____

_____

vocation

job; calling (n)

Despite working as a construction worker for ten years, he felt his true vocation was nursing and returned to school to follow his dreams.

Your sentence:

_____

_____

_____

_____

_____

_____

vulgar

offensive (adj)

Vulgar language was not tolerated in school.

Your sentence:

_____

_____

_____

_____

_____

_____

wane

become smaller
or less intense (v)

The king's power waned once his son took over the throne.

Your sentence:

_____

_____

_____

_____

_____

_____

wary

lacking complete trust (adj)

The investor was wary about investing so much money in a single company.

Your sentence:

_____

_____

_____

_____

_____

_____

wily

able to gain an advantage (adj)

She was a wily opponent, able to use her competitors' weaknesses against them.

Your sentence:

_____

_____

_____

_____

_____

_____

wrath

extreme anger (n)

He made sure to finish his weekly chores, fearing his mother's wrath if he did otherwise.

Your sentence:

_____

_____

_____

_____

_____

_____

Made in United States
North Haven, CT
08 September 2023

41286386R00143